The
Friendship
Garden

Artwork by
Lori Siebert

HARVEST HOUSE PUBLISHERS
EUGENE, OREGON

The Friendship Garden

Text Copyright © 2009 by Harvest House Publishers
Artwork Copyright by Lori Siebert

Published by Harvest House Publishers
Eugene, Oregon 97402
www.harvesthousepublishers.com

ISBN 978-0-7369-2432-0

Written by Georgia Varozza

Courtney Davis, Inc.
340 Main Street
Franklin, Tennessee 37064

www.courtneydavis.com

Design and production by Garborg Design Works, Savage, Minnesota

Printed in China

12 13 14 15 / LP / 10 9 8 7 6

Contents

New Friends 5

Old Friends 13

True Friends 23

Two's Company 33

A Bouquet of Friendship 45

I'm There for You 55

You have to
sow before you
can reap.

ROBERT COLLIER

New Friends

The spring garden delights us. Tender new shoots begin to push through the soil, promising a future of vibrant color and sweet fragrance. It's a happy time! We carefully nurture these fragile plants, helping them to withstand the spring storms we know will come. We hope that under our care, our gardens will grow strong and produce well.

New friends need the same care.

We meet someone and just know…this is a kindred spirit! The future is bright with promise, but we have work to do. We water our friendships by spending time together, fertilize the connection with kind words and actions, and weed out anything that hinders growth. The storms of life will come as surely as the spring brings rain, and our friendships will be tested. But like our carefully tended spring gardens, a well-cared-for friendship will weather these storms and be stronger and more beautiful for them.

Friends are like melons; shall I tell you why?
To find one good you must one hundred try.

CLAUDE MERMET

Go often to the house of thy friend,
for weeds choke the unused path.

RALPH WALDO EMERSON

things happen for a reason...
just believe!

Since there is nothing so well worth having

as friends, never lose a chance to make them.

FRANCESCO GUICCIARDINI

A true
friend is
one of
life's
greatest
blessings

How rare and wonderful is that flash of a moment
when we realize we have discovered a friend.

WILLIAM ROTSLER

A hug is worth a thousand words.
A friend is worth more.

AUTHOR UNKNOWN

Friendship is born at that moment when
one person says to another, "What! You
too? I thought I was the only one."

C.S. LEWIS

When I count
my blessings,
I count
YOU
twice!

Old Friends

Summer settles in and the fullness of an established garden is dazzling. Plants prettily display their riot of colors, and it can be hard to tell where one ends and another begins, so dense and intertwined is the growth.

Old friendships boast these same qualities. We finish each other's sentences, laugh at the same silly jokes, and lean upon the other when our own strength gives out. The long period of cultivation in old friendships reaps a rich harvest.

Constant use had not worn ragged
the fabric of their friendship.

DOROTHY PARKER

It takes a long time to grow an old friend.

JOHN LEONARD

14

Wishing to be friends is quick work, but friendship is a slow-ripening fruit.

ARISTOTLE

Friendship does not spring up and grow great and become perfect all at once, but requires time and the nourishment of thoughts.

DANTE

15

Oh, the comfort—the inexpressible comfort of feeling *safe* with a person—having neither to weigh thoughts nor measure words, but pouring them all right out, just as they are, chaff and grain together; certain that a faithful hand will take and sift them, keep what is worth keeping, and then with the breath of kindness blow the rest away.

DINAH CRAIK

Those who bring sunshine
to the lives of others
cannot keep it from themselves.

SIR JAMES M. BARRIE

17

What a relief it is to see your

friendly smile!

JACOB, THE BOOK OF GENESIS

19

The best mirror is an old friend.

GEORGE HERBERT

The best kind of friend is the one you could sit on a porch with, never saying a word, and walk away feeling like that was the best conversation you'd had.

AUTHOR UNKNOWN

True Friends

Perennial flowers come back year after year, true to form. They burst into bloom and then disappear during fall and winter. But we know these gorgeous flowers will be back, more stunning than before, and so we leave a space in our gardens just for them.

True friends are always there as well. Like perennials, we may lose sight of them for a time, but we leave a space in our hearts just for them. They will be back, and our times together will be sweet…true to form and more delightful than ever.

Best friends are the ones who can be the farthest away but there the fastest when you call.

AUTHOR UNKNOWN

May God's love and the Holy
Spirit's friendship be yours.

THE BOOK OF SECOND CORINTHIANS

True friendship is a plant of slow growth, and must
undergo and withstand the shocks of adversity
before it is entitled to the appellation.

GEORGE WASHINGTON

A true friend is always loyal.

THE BOOK OF PROVERBS

26

One measure of
friendship consists not
in the number of things
friends can discuss, but in
the number of things they
need no longer mention.

CLIFTON FADIMAN

27

It is only with the heart that
one can see rightly; what is
essential is invisible to the eye.

ANTOINE DE SAINT-EXUPERY

A person is only beautiful
when their own beauty is
reflecting onto others.

TARA GRADY

you make the world a better place just by being in it.

29

If we would build on a sure foundation
in friendship, we must love friends for
their sake rather than for our own.

CHARLOTTE BRONTE

The best things in life are nearest: Breath in your
nostrils, light in your eyes, flowers at your feet,
duties at your hand, the path of right just before you.
Then do not grasp at the stars, but do life's plain,
common work as it comes, certain that daily duties
and daily bread are the sweetest things in life.

ROBERT LOUIS STEVENSON

Two's Company

Gardeners seem to love the number two: there are peas and carrots, tomatoes and basil, cucumbers and dill, roses and garlic. Yes! Roses and garlic are great companions in the garden. Planted together, the garlic acts as a foil for pesky aphids and other pests, and the roses are then free to grow and bloom profusely.

God plants companions in our lives as well. They can be anyone, but the key is that we understand that they make a positive difference in our lives. Our companions help us to thrive. Oh, we could exist without them, but God in His infinite wisdom gives us the pleasure of companions that He plants right into our hearts…just like roses and garlic.

Two are better than one, because they have a good return for their work: If one falls down, his friend can help him up.

THE BOOK OF ECCLESIASTES

If you live to be 100, I hope I live to be 100 minus 1 day, so I never have to live without you.

WINNIE THE POOH

Walking with a friend in the dark is better

...man walking alone in the light.

HELEN KELLER

I have learned that to
have a good friend is the
purest of all God's gifts,
for it is a love that has no
exchange of payment.

FRANCES FARMER

The most I can do
for my friend is
simply be his friend.

HENRY DAVID THOREAU

We are all travelers in the wilderness
of this world, and the best we can find
in our travels is an honest friend.

ROBERT LOUIS STEVENSON

Happiness isn't the easiest thing to
find, but one place you're guaranteed
to find it is in a friend's smile.

ALLISON POLER

Give me one friend,
just one, who meets
the needs of all my
varying moods.

ESTHER M. CLARK

Are we not like two volumes of one book?

Marceline Desbordes-Valmore

Books, like friends,
should be few
and well chosen.

SAMUEL PATTERSON

41

Things are never quite as scary when you have a best friend.

BILL WATTERSON

The rule of friendship means there should be mutual sympathy between them, each supplying what the other lacks and trying to benefit the other, always using friendly and sincere words.

MARCUS TULLIUS CICERO

friends don't get any better than you

44

A Bouquet of Friendship

Have you ever thought that a bouquet of flowers is just like our friendships? They come in all shapes and sizes.

There are roses, with thorns that can wound but with blooms so beautiful to look at and smell that we overlook their barbs. Or violets, whose dainty petals do best in a quiet, shady corner of the garden. Marigolds are extravagantly colorful and thrive even with little attention. Or how about multitalented nasturtiums, whose round speckled leaves and edible blossoms are showy in the garden and tasty in a salad. And you can't help but notice sunflowers, those standouts in any garden. Taller than most plants, they are always turning their faces to the sun as if to shout, "Look at me!"

Life is nicer with a big bouquet of friends…each "bloom" distinctive and irreplaceable, one part of a perfect whole.

Best friends are a special bouquet picked by the hand of God.

AUTHOR UNKNOWN

Plant a seed of
friendship;
reap a bouquet of
happiness.

LOIS L. KAUFMAN

dig

flower bud

soil

The language of

46

seed

SEEDS

tulips

earth

om

plant

friendship is not words but meanings.

HENRY DAVID THOREAU

I cannot even imagine where I
would be today were it not for that
handful of friends who have given
me a heart full of joy. Let's face it,
friends make life a lot more fun.

CHARLES R. SWINDOLL

If friends
were flowers,
I'd pick you.

AUTHOR UNKNOWN

49

Do not protect
yourself by a
fence, but rather
by your friends.

CZECH PROVERB

My friends
are my estate.

EMILY DICKINSON

50

God almighty first planted a
garden. And indeed, it is the
purest of human pleasures.

FRANCIS BACON

make a
little
garden
out of
life!

I awoke with devout thanksgiving for my friends.

RALPH WALDO EMERSON

But friendship is precious, not only in the shade, but in the sunshine of life; and thanks to a benevolent arrangement of things, the greater part of life is sunshine.

THOMAS JEFFERSON

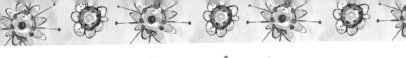

I'm There for You

Flowers help us speak and listen to the language of the heart. A beautiful floral arrangement, sent at the right time, speaks clearly to the recipient. And no matter what the occasion—no matter what the accompanying card says—what we hear is, "You matter to me." "I love you."

It's a gift that goes far beyond the bouquet itself. Flowers can cheer us on, mark important moments in life, pave the way for restoration, or remind us who our friends are. Whether stately roses, fragrant lilies, or even a bunch of wildflowers hastily picked along the side of a lane, each stem in a proffered bouquet proclaims the words friends say to one another: "I'm there for you."

Let us be grateful to people who make us happy. They are the charming gardeners who make our souls blossom.

MARCEL PROUST

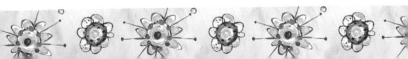

Friendship is a sheltering tree.

SAMUEL TAYLOR COLERIDGE

You can't stay in your corner of the forest waiting for others to come to you. You have to go to them sometimes.

WINNIE THE POOH

56

Grow flowers of gratitude
in the soil of prayer.

VERBENA WOODS

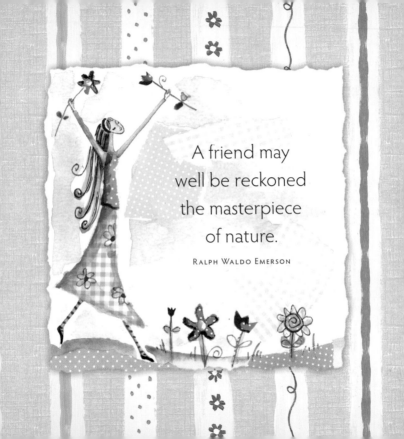

A friend may
well be reckoned
the masterpiece
of nature.

RALPH WALDO EMERSON

Friendship isn't a big thing—
it's a million little things.

AUTHOR UNKNOWN

It is a sweet thing, friendship, a dear balm,
A happy and auspicious bird of calm.

SHELLY

Friendship is one of the sweetest joys of life.
Many might have failed beneath the bitterness
of their trial had they not found a friend.

CHARLES HADDON SPURGEON.

Kind words can be short
and easy to speak, but their
echoes are truly endless.

MOTHER TERESA

Nothing but heaven itself is better
than a friend who is really a friend.

PLAUTUS

A single rose
can be my garden...
a single friend,
my world.

LEO BUSCAGLIA